Zombie cupcakes

Zilly Rosen

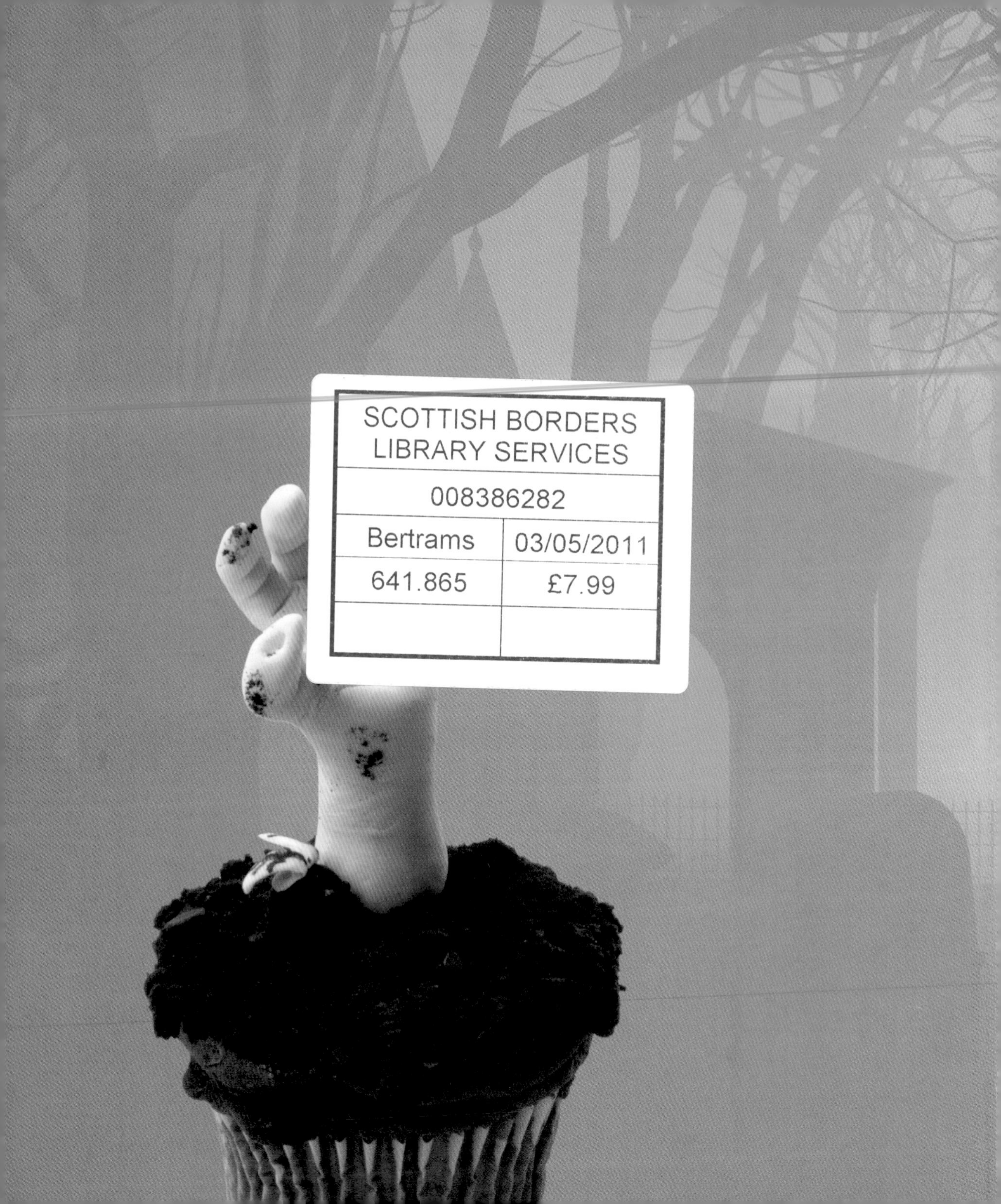

Zombie
cupcakes

Zilly Rosen

Ivy Press

First published in the UK in 2010 by
Ivy Press
210 High Street, Lewes
East Sussex BN7 2NS, UK
www.ivy-group.co.uk

Copyright © Ivy Press Limited 2010

British Library Cataloguing-in-Publication Data
A catalogue record for this book is available from the British Library.

ISBN: 978-1-907332-27-2

Ivy Press
This book was conceived, designed, and produced by Ivy Press
Creative Director **Peter Bridgewater**
Publisher **Jason Hook**
Editorial Director **Tom Kitch**
Senior Designer **James Lawrence**
Editors **Susanna Tee** and **Jo Richardson**
Designer **Glyn Bridgewater**
Photographer **Michelle Zurowski**
Illustrator **Sarah Skeate**

The author would like to thank Hannah Russell for all her artistic contributions and tireless labour on the book, and the fearless Shannon Pilarski, whose knowledge of all things zombie is only exceeded by her creativity and her sculpting ability. Without Shannon, the undead decorations in this book would never have come to life.

The publisher would like to thank the following for permission to reproduce copyright material: Fotolia/AlienCat: 2; Gabrel: 16; Imyme: 16; Dmytro Konstantynov: 20; Andreas Gradin: 24, 26; Alexei Novikov: 28; Steven Smith: 32; Sergey: 36; Ivan Bliznetsov: 38, 44; lassedesignen: 40; fotoundmakeup: 42; Mary Lan: 52; Shutterstock/Cajoer: 3; Fribus Ekaterina: 18; iStockphoto/Joshua Blake: 6.

Printed in China

Colour origination by Ivy Press Reprographics

10 9 8 7 6 5 4 3 2 1

Notes for the Reader

This book uses both metric and imperial measurements; use only one system rather than mixing metric and imperial. Teaspoon measurements are assumed to be 5 ml and tablespoons are assumed to be 15 ml. Milk is assumed to be full fat unless otherwise stated.

Pregnant and breastfeeding women are advised to avoid eating peanuts and peanut products. Ready-made ingredients used in the recipes in this book may contain nuts – sufferers from nut allergies should check any ingredients' packaging before use.

contents

introduction

Zombies are on the march. It is too late to turn them back. Their animated corpses are shambling out of the graveyards and taking over every aspect of popular culture before our very eyes. Vying for world domination with another undead creature, the timeless and seductive vampire, the zombie is resurrecting itself and infecting armies of devoted followers in comics, video games, films and television, and even in 'mash-ups' of the novels of Jane Austen: who is no doubt turning in her grave. So what exactly are zombies, and why are they now emerging through the cracked icing of that other irresistible craze, the cupcake?

Well, the flesh-eating undead can be traced back to ancient mythology and to the infamous voodoo traditions of Haiti, but the modern zombie is generally considered to have risen from *Night of the Living Dead*, the horror film made in 1968 by the legendary director George A. Romero. Here, we encounter the characteristic slow-moving army of plague-infested ghouls that threatens to overwhelm the human race, giving birth to the dead-eyed, rotting creature that now has its own genre. Certainly, the popularity of zombies in books and movies rises and falls, but like the creatures themselves they just keep on coming; and they are currently, without question, on the march. And what better way to celebrate zombies than with another phenomenon which has refused to die down, defying its critics and its nature to become bigger and bigger, and spawning culinary followers from celebrity chefs to café owners around the globe? The cupcake bar might not immediately seem the natural home of the zombie, but who said that these delicious little creations all had to be universally cute? Whether you wish to finally find a party food that does justice to Halloween horror, to bake a bitesize offering that was just made for trick or treating, or simply to create fashionable and soul-stirring party cupcakes that will have your legions of guests marching on the kitchen to ask for more, the time is undeniably ripe for cupcakes to rise from their graves of cuteness and reveal their dark hearts. Putting the sickly into the sweet taste of these delicious treats, *Zombie Cupcakes* offers you a sugar-coated carnage of body parts, graveyards, and rotting monsters that will ensure adults and children alike squeal in delighted horror before sinking their teeth into the iced flesh and realizing that zombies never tasted so good. Welcome to the graveyard of traditional cupcakes. Enter at your own risk...

Delicious Eye Popper cupcakes are the perfect treat to usher in your guests.

The cupcakes in this book use a variety of basic recipes for the decorations and toppings. The quantity of each basic recipe used varies from cupcake to cupcake, so check the cupcake recipe before you start. You may wish to make a smaller batch of the basic recipes, or you can store the leftovers for use with other cupcakes. Bear in mind that the basic recipes don't all keep for the same amount of time.

White fondant can easily be bought from specialized cake-decorating shops or suppliers, along with a variety of different colours. However, if you have difficulty buying coloured fondant, you can colour it yourself. Half and Half (see page 11) can be coloured in the same way.

Many decorations need to be cut using a craft knife. Take the same care when using a craft knife to cut the decorations as you would when cutting paper, and make sure you keep it out of the reach of children.

dark chocolate ganache

Makes enough to cover 12–14 cupcakes

- 475 g/1 lb 1 oz mini plain chocolate chips
- 540 ml/19 fl oz double cream
- 5 g/⅛ oz unsalted butter

1 Put the chocolate chips in a large heatproof bowl. Bring the cream to the boil in a saucepan.

2 Before the bubbles reach the top of the pan, pour the cream into the chocolate chips and whisk together until smooth.

3 Add the butter and stir until smooth and shiny. Place clingfilm directly over the surface to prevent a skin from forming, then leave at room temperature overnight to cool. Store in the refrigerator, covered, for up to three weeks.

Italian meringue buttercream

Makes enough to cover 12–14 cupcakes

- 225 g/8 oz granulated sugar
- 50 ml/2 fl oz water
- 6 large egg whites
- 350 g/12 oz unsalted butter, softened, cut into small pieces
- 1 tsp pure vanilla extract
- pinch of salt

flavours

chocolate: 85 g/3 oz plain chocolate, melted
caramel: 6 tsp dulce de leche and ⅛ tsp salt
coffee: 3 tsp instant espresso powder dissolved in 1 tsp boiling water
amaretto: ½–1 tsp almond extract
coconut: 1 tsp coconut extract and 3 tsp coconut milk

1 Put the sugar and water in a large saucepan and stir together. Bring to a rolling boil on high heat, then boil undisturbed for 5 minutes.

2 Allow the sugar mixture to continue boiling while you put the egg whites in the bowl of a large freestanding electric whisk and whisk on high until stiff.

3 Continuing to whisk on high, carefully hold the pan with the sugar syrup well above the bowl and slowly pour the syrup into the egg whites in a thin stream, without allowing it to touch the whisk.

4 Continue to whisk the egg white mixture on high for 10 minutes until cool.

5 With the machine still running, add the pieces of butter and mix until combined.

6 Reduce the speed to low, add the vanilla extract and salt and continue to whisk until combined.

7 To flavour the buttercream, add the ingredients for your chosen flavour at the end of whisking.

8 Store in the refrigerator, covered, for up to three weeks or in small amounts in the freezer for up to three months. Before use, return to room temperature and then beat until smooth and the texture is restored.

royal icing

cream cheese
frosting

Makes enough to cover 12 cupcakes

- 350 g/12 oz cream cheese, at room temperature
- 55 g/2 oz unsalted butter, softened
- ½ tsp pure vanilla extract
- 85 g/3 oz icing sugar
- pinch of salt
- ¼ tsp lemon juice

1 Put the cream cheese and butter in a large bowl and beat with a wooden spoon until soft and light. Add the vanilla extract and mix together.

2 Sift in the icing sugar and salt, add the lemon juice and mix together until well combined. Store in the refrigerator, covered, for up to three days.

Makes about 225 g/8 oz

- 1 large egg white, plus extra if necessary
- pinch of cream of tartar
- 200–225 g/7–8 oz icing sugar, sifted
- paste food colouring (optional)

1 Put the egg white and cream of tartar in the bowl of a large freestanding electric whisk and whisk together until frothy.

2 With the machine still running, gradually add the icing sugar until the mixture begins to stiffen and turn opaque white. Scrape down the side of the bowl and whisk briefly on high. The mixture should be stiff but still pliable.

3 If necessary, thin the mixture with a little extra egg white or a drop of food colouring. Cover with a damp tea towel to prevent a crust from forming. To store, put it in a container, place clingfilm directly over the surface to prevent a skin from forming and seal the container. Keep in the refrigerator for up to one week.

4 To colour the icing, add the appropriate paste food colouring in drops or on a cocktail stick or the tip of a knife and beat in until you achieve the required colour.

piping gel
'blood'

Makes about 85 g/3 oz

- 85 g/3 oz clear piping gel
- 4–5 drops red paste food colouring

1 Put the piping gel in a small bowl, add the paste food colouring in drops or on a cocktail stick or the tip of a knife and beat in until you achieve a deep blood red colour. Store according to the instructions on the packet.

half & half

Makes about 225 g/8 oz

- 115 g/4 oz shop-bought white fondant
- 115 g/4 oz ready-to-use gum paste
- white vegetable fat (optional)

1 Knead the fondant and then the gum paste separately on a work surface until smooth, then combine and knead until well mixed. If the mixture becomes sticky, add a little white vegetable fat.

2 Cover with an upturned bowl or cup to prevent a crust from forming. To store, roll the mixture into a ball, double wrap in clingfilm and keep in a sealed container at room temperature for up to two weeks.

rolling out half & half for cupcake toppers

- acetate sheets (available from art and crafts or cake-decorating shops or suppliers)
- white vegetable fat, for sticking and greasing
- Half and Half (see left)

1 Cut a strip of acetate to the size directed by the recipe. Put white vegetable fat under the strip to stick it to the work surface and grease the strip liberally with more fat.

2 Place the Half and Half on the acetate and roll out very thinly to a thickness of 3 mm/⅛ inch or less. Using a craft knife, cut as directed in the recipe. Leave to dry overnight.

colouring fondant & half & half

- shop-bought white fondant or Half and Half (see page left)
- white vegetable fat, for greasing
- drops of paste food colouring (as directed by the recipe)

1 Add as many drops of paste food colouring as directed by the recipe. When instructed to add a dab of colouring, use the end of a cocktail stick to pick up a very small amount of colouring, then mix it in the fondant or Half and Half.

2 Lightly grease the work surface with a little white vegetable fat and knead the mixture until evenly coloured. If necessary, add a little vegetable fat to the icing to prevent it from becoming sticky. Add more food colouring as needed until the colour is the desired shade.

zombie bits & pieces

Many of the cupcake recipes in this book have extra decorative details. We've included a selection of ideas here, from maggots and flies to improvised weapons for fighting back the zombie hordes. Some recipes suggest the most appropriate decorations for you to use, but obviously you're free to add them to any of the recipes in the book or to use them to decorate your own zombie cupcake creations.

When you're hosting a party, you could scatter these bits and pieces between the cupcakes if you're presenting the cupcakes as an ensemble, or if you're presenting a larger spread of food then perhaps dot them around the table on napkins.

teeth

Makes 12

- 40 g/1½ oz plain white Half and Half (see page 11)

1 Roll the Half and Half into 12 oval shapes. Make a cut in the middle of the oval that extends halfway up to create the roots. Pinch the ends of the roots to a point.

2 Use the side of a cocktail stick to indent 2 criss-crossed lines on the rounded end of the tooth. Use the end of the cocktail stick to make additional creases and crevices so that the tooth looks like a molar.

3 Press the side of the cocktail stick all the way around the tooth to make the groove that separates the tooth from the root. Repeat to make another 11 teeth. Leave to dry overnight. Store in a cool, dry place, but not in the refrigerator.

maggots

Makes 12

- 10–15 g/¼–½ oz plain white Half and Half (see page 11)

1 Roll the Half and Half into a ball and then pinch off tiny amounts. Roll between your finger and thumb into small lengths. Leave to dry overnight. Store in a cool, dry place, but not the refrigerator.

tombstones
& crosses

Makes 6 of each

- 1½ tsp instant espresso powder
- ½ tsp boiling water
- 300 g/10½ oz white plain, cake or pastry flour, plus extra for dusting
- 50 g/1¾ oz cocoa powder
- pinch of salt
- 225 g/8 oz unsalted butter, softened
- 200 g/7 oz granulated sugar
- 1 large egg
- 2 tsp pure vanilla extract
- 50 g/1¾ oz plain white Royal Icing, for decorating (see page 10; optional)

1 Preheat the oven to 160°C/150°C fan/ 325°F/Gas Mark 3. Line a baking sheet with baking paper. Dissolve the espresso powder in the boiling water. Sift the flour, cocoa powder and salt together.

2 Put the butter and sugar in a large bowl and, using an electric whisk, beat together until pale in colour. Add the egg, vanilla extract and espresso liquid and mix together until combined.

3 Add the sifted ingredients to the mixture, in 3 equal batches, and mix until just blended. Wrap the dough in clingfilm and chill in the refrigerator for about 1 hour.

4 Roll the dough out on a lightly floured work surface to a thickness of 3–5 mm/⅛–¼ inch. Using a sharp knife, cut 2 long strips of dough 1 cm/½ inch wide, then cut into strips 12 cm/4½ inches long. From the remaining dough, cut out 6 rectangles 5 x 4 cm/2 x 1½ inches.

5 To make the tombstones, cut the top off each rectangle in a curve. Transfer the rectangles to the prepared baking sheet.

6 To make the crosses, place a strip of dough on the baking sheet. Cut two 2.5 x 1-cm/1 x ½-inch pieces from another strip of dough. Press the 2 smaller pieces onto either side of the long strip about a third of the way down. Make sure that the dough is touching so that the parts will bake together and come out as a single shape.

7 Bake in the oven for 10–12 minutes, turning the cookies once, until set but not dark on the edges. Leave to cool for 30 minutes.

8 If wished, fit a piping bag or a baking paper cone with a fine plain piping nozzle and fill with the Royal Icing. Pipe the names of people you know or great zombie movie directors on the tombstones.

rats

Makes 2

- 25 g/1 oz Half and Half, coloured black with 3 drops black paste food colouring (see page 11)
- 25 g/1 oz Royal Icing, coloured red with 4 drops red paste food colouring (see page 10)

flies

Makes 12

- 40 g/1½ oz Half and Half, coloured black with 4 drops black paste food colouring (see page 11)
- 25 g/1 oz plain white Half and Half
- 25 g/1 oz Royal Icing, coloured red with 4 drops red paste food colouring (see page 10)
- red edible marker pen
- black edible marker pen

1 Divide the black Half and Half into 12 small balls and then shape into ovals for the bodies. Divide the white Half and Half into 24 small ovals for the wings. Pinch the ovals flat.

2 Press an oval down on the handle of a wooden spoon to curve, angling inwards. Press a second oval down on the spoon so that it overlaps the first, angling inwards from the opposite side. Use a little water to join the wings where they overlap. Repeat to make 11 more pairs of wings. Leave to set for about 10 minutes.

3 When the wings have set, curve the joined edge under to create a surface to attach to the body. Use a little water to attach the wings to the centre of the body.

4 Use a small amount of red Royal Icing in a piping bag or baking paper cone fitted with a fine plain piping nozzle to pipe 2 eyes on the fly. Use the edible marker pens to make lines on the wings. Repeat to make the other 11 flies. Leave to dry overnight. Store in a cool, dry place, but not in the refrigerator.

1 Roll most of the Half and Half into 2 balls. Pinch one end into a small point to make the rat's nose. Pull and pinch the other end to make an elongated, thin tail. To make the head appear separate from the body, take the side of a cocktail stick and roll it around the Half and Half where the neck would be. Repeat to make another rat.

2 To make the ears, roll the remaining Half and Half into 4 tiny balls and squeeze them flat. Use a small amount of water to attach the ears to the rats' heads. Use the cocktail stick to smooth the area where they join if your fingers seem too big.

3 Fit a piping bag or a baking paper cone with a fine plain piping nozzle and fill with the red Royal Icing. Pipe 2 beady eyes on either side of each head. Leave to dry overnight. Store in a cool, dry place, but not in the refrigerator.

knives

Makes 12

- 55 g/2 oz Half and Half, coloured grey with 1 drop black paste food colouring (see page 11)
- 15 g/½ oz Half and Half, coloured brown with 3 drops brown paste food colouring
- 25 g/1 oz plain white Royal Icing (see page 10)

1 Roll out the grey Half and Half very thinly on an acetate strip greased with white vegetable fat. Cut 6 rectangles, each measuring 13 x 25 mm/½ x 1 inch. Cut diagonally across each rectangle to create 2 triangular knife blades.

2 Roll out the brown Half and Half very thinly on an acetate strip greased with white vegetable fat. Cut into a rectangle measuring 13 x 25 mm/½ x 1 inch. Cut in half lengthways, then make 5 evenly spaced vertical cuts to make knife handles.

3 Using the white Royal Icing in a piping bag or baking paper cone fitted with a fine plain piping nozzle, attach a knife handle to the corner of each knife blade. Pipe 2 dots on each handle to represent rivets. Leave to dry overnight. Store in a cool, dry place, but not in the refrigerator.

baseball bats

Makes 4

- 70 g/2½ oz Half and Half, coloured pale brown with 1 drop brown and 1 drop yellow paste food colouring (see page 11)

1 Roll the Half and Half into 4 thin sausage shapes that are thicker at one end and gradually becomes thinner at the other end. Cut the thinner end so that it is blunt. Push the blunt end to create the handle of the bat.

2 Use a cocktail stick, rolled on the edge, to define the handle of the bat further. Repeat to make another 3 bats. Leave to dry overnight. Store in a cool, dry place, but not in the refrigerator.

crowbars

Makes 4

- 25 g/1 oz Half and Half, coloured black with 3 drops black paste food colouring (see page 11)

1 Roll the Half and Half into 4 thin sausage shapes. A quarter of the way down, bend the sausage shape at a right angle, then pinch the short end flat.

2 Use a craft knife to cut a 'V' out of the flat end of the crowbar. Repeat to make another 3 crowbars. Leave to dry overnight. Store in a cool, dry place, but not in the refrigerator.

shovels

Makes 4

- 40 g/1½ oz Half and Half, coloured grey with a dab of black paste food colouring (see page 11)
- 40 g/1½ oz Half and Half, coloured pale brown with 1 drop brown and 1 drop yellow paste food colouring

1 Roll the grey Half and Half into 4 balls. Squeeze into a triangle shape. Flatten the triangle to create the blade of the shovel. Pinch the edges so that it appears to be sharp, especially at the point.

2 Roll the pale brown Half and Half into a thin sausage shape 7.5 cm/3 inches long. Flatten one end and attach it to the back of the shovel blade with water. Repeat to make another 3 shovels. Leave to dry overnight. Store in a cool, dry place, but not in the refrigerator.

DIFFICULTY RATING

MAKES **12**

Decorations can be made the same day as baking

red velvet
cupcakes

- 125 ml/4 fl oz buttermilk
- ½ tsp pure vanilla extract
- ½ tsp distilled malt vinegar
- 3 tsp red liquid food colouring
- 115 g/4 oz unsalted butter, softened
- 150 g/5½ oz granulated sugar
- 2 large eggs, beaten
- 200 g/7 oz white plain, cake or pastry flour
- 3 tsp cocoa powder
- ½ tsp bicarbonate of soda
- ¼ tsp salt

All it takes is just one bite from a zombie and you will turn into one of the undead. This red velvet cupcake, on the other hand, is so delicious that you won't be able to stop at one bite – instead you will keep on munching until you have devoured the whole thing. The blood oozing out of the bite mark is red piping gel.

decorations

- 1 drop peach paste food colouring
- 1 quantity Italian Meringue Buttercream (see page 8)
- 125 g/4½ fl oz Piping Gel 'Blood' (see page 10)
- 12 Teeth (see page 12)

toxic bite

1 Preheat the oven to 190°C/170°C fan/ 375°F/Gas Mark 5. Line a 12-hole muffin tin with 12 large paper baking cases. Put the buttermilk, vanilla extract, vinegar and red liquid food colouring in a bowl and mix together.

2 Put the butter and sugar in a large bowl and, using an electric whisk, beat together until pale and fluffy. Gradually add the eggs and beat well together. Sift in the flour, cocoa powder, bicarbonate of soda and salt and mix together. Add the buttermilk mixture and stir together until combined. Spoon the mixture into the paper cases. Bake for about 20 minutes, turning once halfway through baking, until well risen and firm to the touch. Transfer to a wire rack and leave to cool.

3 Meanwhile, make the decorations. Add the peach food colouring to the Italian Meringue Buttercream in drops or on the end of a cocktail stick and mix well together until evenly coloured. When the cupcakes are cold, spread or pipe the icing on top of the cupcakes. (If you freeze the iced cupcakes briefly, it will allow you to scrape the icing very smoothly with a small spatula.)

4 To create a bite on one side of each cupcake, begin by pressing the small end of a large plain piping nozzle into the icing 5 to 7 times in a curve across the edge of the cake.

5 Use the piping nozzle to drag away the remaining icing in the bite area to create a lower level of icing.

6 Fill in the bite with Piping Gel 'Blood'. Bring some of the gel down the side of the cupcake so that it forms a pool on the plate or table.

7 Use a cocktail stick to stir some of the buttercream into the gel in the middle of the bite to create a paler area.

8 Using a piping bag or baking paper cone fitted with a fine plain piping nozzle, pipe the remaining gel onto the root of each tooth and then lay the tooth in the pool of 'blood' that has dripped off the cupcake.

know your
zombie

What was the cause of infection in the film *28 Days Later* (2002)?

1 Infected water supply

2 Infected lab chimpanzees

3 Infected blood transfusion

(The answer is on page 80.)

t-virus

DIFFICULTY RATING

MAKES **12**

Make the decorations the day
before baking

blue banana
cupcakes

- 1 very ripe banana
- 1 tsp lemon juice
- 115 g/4 oz unsalted butter, softened
- 200 g/7 oz granulated sugar
- 3 large eggs, beaten
- ½ tsp grated lemon rind
- 6 tsp soured cream
- 1 tsp blue liquid food colouring
- 1 tsp blue curaçao liqueur (optional)
- 200 g/7 oz white plain, cake or pastry flour
- 1 tsp baking powder
- ¼ tsp bicarbonate of soda
- ¼ tsp salt

In the film *Resident Evil* (2002), the cause of the zombie
onslaught is the T-Virus that is accidentally released, infecting
the entire research facility where it was being developed. Dare to
release this yummy cupcake version into your own system and
see what happens. The recommended antidote, if you should
need it, is a drop of green food colouring in a glass of cold milk.

decorations

- 85 g/3 oz plain white Half and Half
  (see page 11)
- 100 g/3½ oz Royal Icing, coloured black
  with 8 drops black paste food colouring
  (see page 10)
- 50 g/1¾ oz Royal Icing, coloured blue with
  1 drop sky blue paste food colouring
- 1 quantity Italian Meringue Buttercream
  (see page 8)
- blue nonpareils, sugar strands or other
  blue cake sprinkles

t-virus

1 The day before, make the decorations. Roll out the Half and Half to make the Cupcake Toppers using a strip of acetate 7.5 x 25 cm/3 x 10 inches (see page 11). Using a craft knife (you can use a straight edge to steady the blade), cut the Half and Half into a strip 4 cm/1½ inches wide.

2 Using the craft knife, cut the Half and Half strip at 2-cm/¾-inch intervals to make 12 small rectangles.

3 Use the tip of the craft knife to cut off the corners of the rectangles and round the short edges into a curve.

4 Put the black Royal Icing in a piping bag or baking paper cone fitted with a fine plain piping nozzle and outline the vial. Add a curved line at the top, and a straight line near the top and the bottom. Repeat for the other vials.

5 Put the blue Royal Icing in a piping bag or baking paper cone fitted with a fine plain piping nozzle and pipe a squiggle down the centre of the middle portion of the vial that curves right, left and then right. Overlap that with a second squiggle that curves left, right and left. Repeat for the other vials. Leave to dry overnight.

6 To make the cupcakes, preheat the oven to 180°C/160°C fan/350°F/Gas Mark 4. Line a 12-hole muffin tin with 12 large paper baking cases. Using a fork, mash the banana with the lemon juice. Put the butter and sugar in a large bowl and, using an electric whisk, beat together until pale and fluffy. Gradually add the eggs and beat well together.

7 Add the mashed banana, lemon rind, soured cream, blue food colouring and blue curaçao, if using, and mix well together. Sift in the flour, baking powder, bicarbonate of soda and salt and mix together. Spoon the mixture into the paper cases. Bake for about 20 minutes, turning once halfway through baking, until well risen and firm to the touch. Transfer to a wire rack and leave to cool.

8 When the cupcakes are cold, spread or pipe the Italian Meringue Buttercream on top of the cupcakes. Place the dry vials on top and sprinkle the entire remaining surface of the buttercream with the blue cake sprinkles.

know your zombie

Name the underground facility where the virus began to spread in *Resident Evil.*

1 The Vault

2 The Lair

3 The Hive

(The answer is on page 80.)

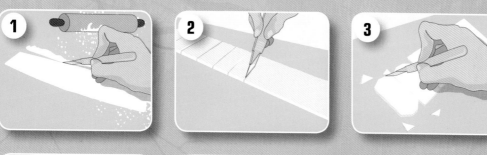

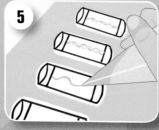

DIFFICULTY RATING

MAKES **12**

Make the decorations the day
before baking

biohazard
ingested

key lime
cupcakes

- 3 large eggs
- 6 tsp vegetable oil
- grated rind of 1 lime and 6 tsp juice
- 100 g/3½ oz unsalted butter, softened
- 200 g/7 oz granulated sugar
- 6 tsp soured cream
- 225 g/8 oz white plain, cake or pastry flour
- ½ tsp baking powder
- ¼ tsp salt

decorations

- 175 g/6 oz Half and Half, coloured orange
  with 6 drops orange paste food colouring
  (see page 11)
- 175 g/6 oz icing sugar
- 6 tsp lime juice
- 2 drops yellow paste food colouring
- 1 dab green paste food colouring

Proper disposal of biohazardous material is absolutely crucial to avoiding an outbreak of the undead. If there are zombies in your midst, someone hasn't been doing their job. Try this sensational key lime cupcake decorated with an orange biohazard symbol. But beware: post consumption, the consumer may have an eerie glow about them, indicating a shift towards the undead.

1 The day before, make the decorations. Roll out a third of the Half and Half to make the Cupcake Toppers using a strip of acetate 7.5 x 20 cm/3 x 8 inches (see page 11).

2 Using a 3-cm/1¼-inch round cutter, cut a circle in the Half and Half. Using a 2.4-cm/⅞-inch round cutter, cut a smaller circle inside the larger circle to make a narrow ring. This will be the centre of the biohazard symbol. Repeat to cut out another 11 rings.

3 Make a template for the biohazard symbol using the photograph on page 24 for reference. Roll out the remaining Half and Half using 2 strips of acetate, each 7.5 x 40 cm/3 x 16 inches (see page 11). Use the template to cut around the edge of the cluster of three rounds. Using the 2.4-cm/⅞-inch round cutter, make a hole in each larger round that just overlaps the centre of the curved edge.

4 Using the small end of a large plain piping nozzle, cut out a small hole in the centre of the symbol. Using a cocktail stick, press a small indented line from the centre circle towards the larger outer circle. Repeat to make another 11 symbols. Leave the rings and symbols to dry overnight.

5 Preheat the oven to 180°C/160°C fan/350°F/Gas Mark 4. Line a 12-hole muffin tin with 12 large paper baking cases. Put the eggs, oil and lime rind and juice in a bowl and whisk together with a whisk.

6 Put the butter and sugar in a large bowl and, using an electric whisk, beat together until pale and fluffy. Blend in the soured cream and then gradually beat in the egg mixture. Sift in the flour, baking powder and salt and mix together. Spoon the mixture into the paper cases. Bake for about 20 minutes, turning once halfway through baking, until well risen and firm to the touch. Transfer to a wire rack and leave to cool.

7 When the cupcakes are cold, make the glaze. Sift the icing sugar into a large bowl and then gradually add the lime juice, stirring until the mixture is smooth and thick enough to coat the back of a wooden spoon. Add the yellow food colouring and, using the end of a cocktail stick, a dab of green food colouring and mix well together until evenly coloured.

8 Dip each cupcake into the glaze so that it is liberally covered. Do not scrape off any extra glaze – drips down the side enhance the look of this cupcake. While the glaze is still wet, place a ring in the centre of each cupcake. Rest a symbol on top of each ring.

know your zombie

The film *The Serpent and the Rainbow* (1988) is based on the non-fiction book of the same name by which anthropologist?

1 Wade Davis

2 Margaret Mead

3 Nancy Scheper-Hughes

(The answer is on page 80.)

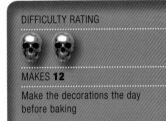

DIFFICULTY RATING

MAKES **12**

Make the decorations the day before baking

the crows

white velvet
cupcakes

- 3 large egg whites
- 175 ml/6 fl oz milk
- ¾ tsp pure vanilla extract
- 350 g/12 oz white plain, cake or pastry flour
- 3 tsp baking powder
- ¼ tsp salt
- 200 g/7 oz granulated sugar
- 125 g/4½ oz unsalted butter, softened

decorations

- cornflour, for dusting
- 350 g/12 oz shop-bought fondant, coloured flesh-coloured with 1–2 drops peach and a dab of blue paste food colouring (see page 11)
- about 175 g/6 oz seedless raspberry jam
- 350 g/12 oz Half and Half, coloured black with 36 drops black paste food colouring (see page 11)
- 25 g/1 oz Royal Icing, coloured red with 4 drops red paste food colouring (see page 10)
- 60 Maggots (see page 12)

This cupcake is inspired by a scene from the movie *28 Days Later*, where a crow sits overhead with a piece of zombie corpse in his mouth. We've chosen a deathly pale skin colour, but you can vary the colour of the fondant to create different flesh tones. The jam and fondant topping contrasts with the subtle flavour of the white velvet cupcake. If you use cocktail sticks to secure the crows, remember to tell your guests.

1 Preheat the oven to 180°C/160°C fan/ 350°F/Gas Mark 4. Line a 12-hole muffin tin with 12 large paper baking cases. Put the egg whites, 2 tablespoons of the milk and the vanilla extract in a medium bowl and mix together with a fork.

2 Sift the flour, baking powder and salt into a large bowl. Stir in the sugar. Add the butter and the remaining milk and, using an electric whisk, beat together until combined. Gradually beat in the egg white mixture. Spoon the mixture into the paper cases. Bake for about 20 minutes, turning once halfway through baking, until well risen and firm to the touch. Transfer to a wire rack and leave to cool.

3 Dust the work surface with cornflour and roll out the fondant to a thickness of 3 mm/⅛ inch. Using a 6.5–7.5-cm/ 2½–2⅞-inch round cutter, cut out 12 rounds that will cover the cupcakes.

4 Use a teaspoon to create an indentation in the centre of each cupcake and spoon 2 teaspoons raspberry jam into each. Cover each jam round with a fondant round.

5 To make the crows, divide the black Half and Half into 12 equal-sized pieces. Reserving a tiny amount for the lower beak, roll one piece of the Half and Half into a ball. Squeeze and pinch the top of the ball to form the head. Squeeze, pinch and flatten the other end of the ball to create the tail. From the head, squeeze and pinch out a long, pointy beak shape. Roll the reserved piece of Half and Half into another beak shape, but curving down at the tip. Attach below the upper beak with water, to make the beak appear open. Repeat to make another 11 crows.

6 With a craft knife, cut a long slit from just inside the edge of the fondant round to 1 cm/½ inch away from the edge on the opposite point of the round. Make a second cut that starts at the same point as the first and is the same length, but ends 5 mm/¼ inch apart from the first cut.

7 Use water to attach the point of the fondant strip to the inside of the crow's beak. Pull up the strip to expose the raspberry jam below.

8 Attach the crow to the fondant round with water. If necessary, anchor the crow to the cupcake with a small piece of cocktail stick. Using a piping bag or baking paper cone fitted with a fine plain piping nozzle, pipe red Royal Icing eyes onto the crow. Use a craft knife to score crow footprints on the fondant. Place the Maggots in the raspberry jam. Repeat to decorate the remaining cupcakes.

know your zombie

What happens after 28 days in the film _28 Days Later_?

1 The zombies start to die of starvation

2 The survivors start to mutate into zombies

3 The zombies turn on each other

(The answer is on page 80.)

DIFFICULTY RATING

MAKES **12**

Make the decorations the day
before baking

zombie moon

devil's food cupcakes

- 55 g/2 oz unsalted butter, softened
- 175 g/6 oz soft dark brown sugar
- 2 large eggs
- 100 g/3½ oz white plain, cake or pastry flour
- ¾ tsp bicarbonate of soda
- 25 g/1 oz cocoa powder
- ¼ tsp salt
- 125 ml/4 fl oz soured cream

decorations

- 3 drops brown paste food colouring
- 3 drops black paste food colouring
- cornflour, for dusting
- 190 g/6½ oz shop-bought fondant, coloured yellow with 3 drops lemon yellow paste food colouring (see page 11)
- lemon extract or vodka, for thinning
- ½ quantity Dark Chocolate Ganache (see page 9)

Your worst nightmare has come true: the zombies are out, they are about to take over the night and they are very hungry. Here they come from behind every tombstone, gnarled tree and fallen cross. Each cupcake is decorated with a zombie rising from the grave, silhouetted against a full moon. This rich devil's food cupcake will help you recognize the enemy and give you the energy to run for your life.

1 The day before, make the decorations. Put the brown and black food colourings in drops or on the end of a cocktail stick onto the lid of an empty jar or plastic container with a raised lip. Mix together with a cocktail stick and leave to dry.

2 Dust the work surface with cornflour and roll out the fondant to a thickness of 3 mm/⅛ inch.

3 Using a 6.5–7.5-cm/2½–2⅞-inch round cutter, cut out 12 rounds that will cover the cupcakes.

4 Pour a small amount of lemon extract or vodka onto the dried food colouring to thin it and mix with a small paintbrush to a painting consistency. Using the photograph on page 32 for inspiration, paint rolling hills, zombies and crosses on the yellow fondant rounds. Leave the paint to dry.

5 To make the cupcakes, preheat the oven to 180°C/160°C fan/350°F/ Gas Mark 4. Line a 12-hole muffin tin with 12 large paper baking cases. Put the butter, sugar, eggs, flour, bicarbonate of soda, cocoa powder and salt in a large bowl and, using an electric whisk, beat together until smooth.

6 Add the soured cream to the mixture and fold in with a large wooden spoon until combined. Spoon the mixture into the paper cases. Bake for 20–25 minutes, turning once halfway through baking, until well risen and firm to the touch. Transfer to a wire rack and leave to cool.

7 When the cupcakes are cold, using a piping bag or baking paper cone fitted with a large plain piping nozzle, pipe a swirl of Dark Chocolate Ganache onto one cupcake.

8 Smooth the swirl with a palette knife or spatula. Place a fondant disc on top of the ganache. Repeat for the remaining cupcakes. Display the cupcakes in a row, to create the illusion of many zombies roaming a graveyard.

know your
zombie

The 1943 film *I Walked with a Zombie* is loosely based on which novel?

1 *Jane Eyre* by Charlotte Brontë (1847)

2 *Frankenstein* by Mary Shelley (1818)

3 *The Premature Burial* by Edgar Allan Poe (1844)

(The answer is on page 80.)

zombie
out
ie will
mud
's
ed
the

DIFFICULTY RATING

MAKES **12**

Make the decorations the day before baking

mud cupcakes

- 10 Oreo cookies
- 50 g/1¾ oz plain chocolate
- 150 g/5½ oz white plain, cake or pastry flour
- ¼ tsp bicarbonate of soda
- ¼ tsp salt
- 70 g/2½ oz unsalted butter, softened
- 150 g/5½ oz granulated sugar
- 2 large eggs, beaten
- ½ tsp pure vanilla extract
- 6 tsp soured cream
- 6 tsp water
- 100 g/3½ oz mini plain chocolate chips

decorations

- 360 g/12½ oz Half and Half, coloured green with 1 drop mint green paste food colouring (see page 11)
- 1 quantity Dark Chocolate Ganache (see page 9)
- 115 g/4 oz chocolate cookies, finely crushed
- 115 g/4 oz mini plain chocolate chips
- a little clear piping gel
- 12 Flies (see page 14)

zombies rising

Take a close look at the graveyard, and you might see a rising from the dead – if you see a rotting hand reaching from underground, you can be sure the rest of the zomb soon follow. They're coming to get you… This delectab cupcake gives you a taste of the grave from the zombie perspective – the earth is made from very finely crushe chocolate cookies. Remember to warn your guests tha hand is secured using a cocktail stick.

zombies rising

1 The day before, make the hands. Roll the green Half and Half into 12 balls and then roll and press one end of each ball to thin it out into a cylinder shape. Flatten the rounded end so that the piece of icing vaguely resembles a ping-pong bat.

2 Using a craft knife, make one cut on one side of the flattened area to make a thumb. Pull it out to the side. Make a second cut in the middle of the remaining rounded portion, and a third and fourth cut on either side to create 4 fingers.

3 Pull and mould the tips of the fingers to make them slightly pointed. Using a cocktail stick, score 3 lines into each finger to create joints. This will be the palm side of the hand. On the reverse side, use the cocktail stick to indent a fingernail shape at the end of each finger.

4 Bend the fingers up from the palm to resemble a claw. Prop the hand against a vertical surface so that it dries in the claw shape. Make another 11 hands in the same way and leave to dry overnight.

5 Preheat the oven to 180°C/160°C fan/ 350°F/Gas Mark 4. Line a 12-hole muffin tin with 12 large paper baking cases. Crush the Oreo cookies into 5-mm/¼-inch pieces. Spoon 1 tablespoon into each paper case, reserving the remaining pieces.

6 Melt the chocolate in a microwave oven on Low or in a heatproof bowl set over a saucepan of gently simmering water. Remove from the heat and leave to cool. Sift the flour, bicarbonate of soda and salt together and set aside. Put the butter and sugar in a large bowl and, using an electric whisk, beat together until pale and fluffy. Blend in the melted chocolate and then gradually beat in the eggs and mix well together. Mix in the vanilla extract and soured cream. Add half the flour mixture and blend in, then mix in the water and remaining flour mixture until incorporated.

7 Spoon half the mixture into the paper cases and spread over the cookies. Add 1 heaped teaspoon of chocolate chips to each. Add the remaining mixture and sprinkle the remaining chocolate chips and cookie pieces over the tops. Bake for about 25 minutes, turning once halfway through baking, until well risen and firm to the touch. Transfer to a wire rack and leave to cool.

8 When the cupcakes are cold, spread or pipe the Dark Chocolate Ganache on top of each cupcake. Mix together most of the chocolate cookie crumbs and all of the chocolate chips in a dish and dip the top of each cupcake into the mixture to create graveyard earth.

9 Push a cocktail stick into the wrist end of each hand and press into the earth to anchor it. To enhance the effect of the hand rising from the grave, paint clear piping gel in different places on the hand and at the base, and sprinkle the remaining chocolate cookie crumbs on the gel so that it sticks. Finish by adding a Fly.

know your zombie

Who directed the 2004 remake of George A Romero's *Dawn of the Dead*?

1 David Cronenberg

2 Zack Snyder

3 Tom Savini

(The answer is on page 80.)

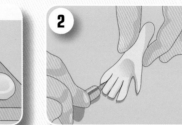

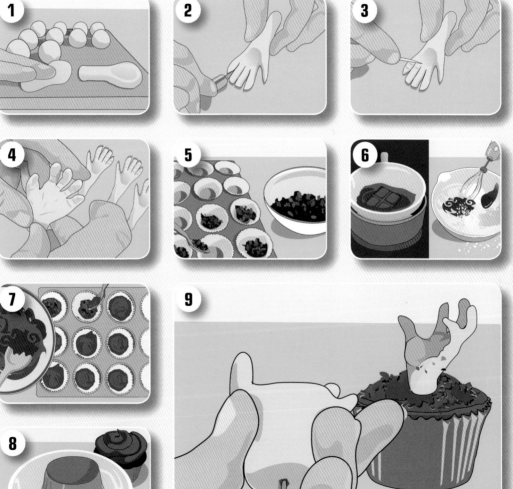

DIFFICULTY RATING

☠

MAKES 24

Make the decorations the day before baking

vanilla cupcakes

- 115 g/4 oz unsalted butter, softened
- 200 g/7 oz granulated sugar
- 3 large eggs, beaten
- 150 ml/5 fl oz milk
- 1 tsp pure vanilla extract
- 225 g/8 oz white plain, cake or pastry flour
- 1½ tsp baking powder
- ¼ tsp salt

chocolate cupcakes

- 115 g/4 oz unsalted butter, softened
- 200 g/7 oz granulated sugar
- 3 large eggs, beaten
- 150 ml/5 fl oz milk
- ½ tsp pure vanilla extract
- 200 g/7 oz white plain, cake or pastry flour
- 25 g/1 oz cocoa powder
- 1½ tsp baking powder
- ¼ tsp salt

trick or treat

'Trick or treat, smell my feet, give me something good to eat.' Sure, kid, here you go! Feeling lucky? You've got about an 80 per cent chance of receiving the treat. If not, better luck next time. Remember to give anyone who bites into a trick one a treat afterwards. We've combined the vanilla and chocolate cupcakes to make layered cupcakes, but you could instead make separate batches of single-flavour cupcakes.

filling

- 20 large marshmallows
- 25 g/1 oz butter or margarine
- a little cold mashed potato

decorations

- cornflour, for dusting
- 675 g/1½ lb shop-bought white fondant
- 250 g/9 oz Piping Gel 'Blood' (see page 10)
- 24 assorted sweets
- Rat, Knife, Tooth and Fly (see pages 12 and 14; optional)

1 Preheat the oven to 180°C/160°C fan/350°F/Gas Mark 4. Line 2 x 12-hole muffin tins with 24 large paper baking cases. To make the Vanilla Cupcakes, put the butter and sugar in a large bowl and, using an electric whisk, beat together until pale and fluffy.

2 Gradually beat the eggs into the mixture, and then stir in the milk and vanilla extract. Sift in the flour, baking powder and salt and fold into the mixture with a large metal spoon. Spoon half of the mixture into 12 of the paper cases and reserve the remainder.

3 To make the Chocolate Cupcakes, put the butter and sugar in a large bowl and, using an electric whisk, beat together until pale and fluffy. Gradually beat in the eggs, and then stir in the milk and vanilla extract. Sift in the flour, cocoa powder, baking powder and salt and fold into the mixture with a large wooden spoon.

4 Spoon half of the mixture into the paper cases, on top of the vanilla mixture. Spoon the other half into the remaining 12 paper cases and top with the reserved vanilla mixture. Bake for about 25 minutes, turning once halfway through baking, until well risen and firm to the touch. Transfer to a wire rack and leave to cool.

5 To fill the cupcakes, use a teaspoon to scoop out a 2.5-cm/1-inch plug from the centre of each cupcake and reserve. Use the teaspoon to remove a little more cake from the holes to make room for the filling.

6 To make the 'treat' filling, put the marshmallows and butter or margarine in a saucepan and heat gently, stirring constantly, until melted. Leave to cool for 5 minutes, then pour the warm mixture into a 30-cm/12-inch disposable piping bag. Pipe the mixture into 20 of the cupcakes. For the 'trick' filling, spoon a little mashed potato into the holes of 4 cupcakes. Replace a reserved cake plug over each filled hole.

7 To decorate the cupcakes, dust the work surface with cornflour and roll out the fondant to a thickness of 3 mm/⅛ inch. Using a 6.5–7.5-cm/2½–2⅞-inch round cutter, cut out 24 rounds to cover the cupcakes.

8 Fit a piping bag or baking paper cone with a fine plain piping nozzle and fill with the Piping Gel 'Blood'. Squeeze the gel into the centre of each fondant round, smearing and dripping as you wish.

9 Place assorted sweets in the pools of gel. If desired, a Rat, Knife, Tooth and Fly can also look very effective when added to a few of the cupcakes.

know your
zombie

What is the name of Shaun and Ed's favourite pub in the film *Shaun of the Dead* (2004)?

1 The Duke of Albany

2 The Winchester

3 The King's Head

(The answer is on page 80.)

DIFFICULTY RATING

MAKES 12

Make the decorations the day before baking

apple sauce & caramel cupcakes

- 115 g/4 oz unsalted butter, softened
- 250 g/9 oz soft light brown sugar
- 2 large eggs, beaten
- 465 g/1 lb ½ oz white plain, cake or pastry flour
- ½ tsp bicarbonate of soda
- 1½ tsp ground cinnamon
- ¼ tsp ground cloves
- ¼ tsp salt
- 140 g/5 oz apple sauce, from a jar
- 1 green apple, peeled, cored and finely chopped
- 12 soft caramels or soft toffees

on the loose

You can chain a zombie down, but there is no guarantee it will stay put for long. With rotten body parts liable to fall off anyway, being a leg down won't worry a zombie if it allows it to escape. This delectable apple cupcake with a caramel or toffee centre begs the question, 'The foot's still here, but where has the rest of my zombie gone off to now?'

decorations

- 360 g/12½ oz Half and Half, coloured green with 1 drop pale green paste food colouring (see page 11)
- 55 g/2 oz plain white Half and Half
- 600 g/1 lb 5 oz Half and Half, coloured grey with 1 drop black paste food colouring
- cornflour, for dusting
- 1 quantity Cream Cheese Frosting (see page 10)
- 20 g/¾ oz Piping Gel 'Blood' (see page 10)

on the loose

1 The day before, make the decorations. To make the foot and leg, roll the pale green Half and Half into 12 balls and use your fingers to roll each ball into a thick log. Bend one end at a 90-degree angle. Pinch and push the bent end into the shape of a foot, pressing the toes flat.

2 Use a craft knife to make a cut at one end of the foot to create the big toe. Cut a small amount off the top of the remaining foot shape to make it slightly shorter. Make 3 cuts at even intervals to create toes. Use a cocktail stick to indent toenail shapes into the tip of each toe.

3 Make a hole in the top of each leg with the handle of a wooden spoon, then use a cocktail stick to tear at the hole to make it look severed. Divide the white Half and Half in two. On a work surface dusted with cornflour, roll each piece into a long sausage shape slightly smaller in diameter than the wooden spoon's handle. Cut each sausage into 6 short, equal lengths and use water to attach one inside each leg to look like exposed bone. Make a slight indentation at the end of the bone for marrow.

4 To make the chains, divide 500 g/ 1 lb 2 oz of the grey Half and Half into 12 equal-sized pieces, then roll each piece into a ball and then into a 25-cm/10-inch long, thin sausage shape. Fold in half, hold one end and twist the 2 lengths together to create a chain.

5 Loop a chain around each foot, leaving one end overlapping the other by 1 cm/ ½ inch, and attach them together with water. Press the 1-cm/½-inch overlap flat and use the small end of a large plain piping nozzle to cut a hole in the centre to allow for a nail.

6 To make the nails, divide the remaining grey Half and Half in half and then roll each half into a long sausage shape thin enough to fit the chain holes. Cut each sausage into 6 short, equal lengths. Press one end of one short length onto the work surface to create a flat top. Use a cocktail stick to score a line across the top, and then make a second score perpendicular to the first. Push the nail through the chain hole. Repeat with the remaining lengths. Leave the decorations to dry overnight.

7 Preheat the oven to 180°C/160°C fan/ 350°F/Gas Mark 4. Line a 12-hole muffin tin with 12 large paper baking cases. Put the butter and sugar in a large bowl and, using an electric whisk, beat together until combined. Gradually beat in the eggs. Sift in the flour, bicarbonate of soda, spices and salt and fold in using a large metal spoon. Fold in the apple sauce and chopped apple.

8 Spoon half the mixture into the paper cases. Place a caramel or toffee in each and then spoon the remaining mixture on top. Bake for about 25 minutes, turning once halfway through baking, until well risen and firm to the touch. Transfer to a wire rack and leave to cool.

9 Not long before serving, ice the cupcakes with the Cream Cheese Frosting. Place a foot, chain and nail on top of each frosted cupcake. Using a piping bag or baking paper cone fitted with a fine plain piping nozzle, pipe Piping Gel 'Blood' in the centre of the bone and at the edge of the ripped skin to enhance the appearance of a severed limb.

know your zombie

Father McGruder says which of the following in *Braindead* (1992)?

1 'I kick ass for the Lord!'

2 'I preach for the Lord!'

3 'I teach for the Lord!'

(The answer is on page 80.)

carrot cupcakes

- 150 ml/5 fl oz vegetable oil
- 3 large eggs
- 175 g/6 oz granulated sugar
- 1 tsp pure vanilla extract
- 200 g/7 oz white plain, cake or pastry flour
- 1½ tsp baking powder
- 1½ tsp ground cinnamon
- ½ tsp ground allspice
- ½ tsp grated nutmeg
- ¼ tsp salt
- 175 g/6 oz grated carrots
- 50 g/1¾ oz chopped walnuts
- 225 g/8 oz canned crushed pineapple

zombies' delights

Zombies deserve a treat every now and then. So serve them up some of these irresistible organ-laden carrot cupcakes and they might not even notice that they are not real body parts. Hopefully, this will give you just a few extra minutes to escape with your own organs intact. For an even wider selection of parts, you could serve these alongside the Brain Food (see page 60) and the Eye Poppers (see page 56).

decorations

- 150 g/5½ oz Half and Half, coloured pink with 1 drop soft pink paste food colouring (see page 11)
- 25 g/1 oz Royal Icing, coloured peach with ½ drop peach paste food colouring (see page 10)
- 25 g/1 oz red Royal Icing, coloured red with 4 drops red paste food colouring
- 25 g/1 oz Royal Icing, coloured blue with 5 drops royal blue paste food colouring

- cornflour, for dusting
- 115 g/4 oz shop-bought fondant, coloured red with 4 drops super red paste food colouring (see page 11)
- 115 g/4 oz shop-bought fondant, coloured black with 8 drops black paste food colouring
- 115 g/4 oz shop-bought fondant, coloured purple with 6 drops regal purple paste food colouring
- 85 g/3 oz clear piping gel

zombies' delights

1 The day before, make 4 lungs, 4 hearts and 4 intestines. For lungs, roll 55 g/2 oz of the pink Half and Half into a ball. Flatten to a disc and cut in half. Squeeze and pinch one inside corner of each half to make lung shaped. Place so that they are almost touching on a sheet of acetate. To make the trachea, roll 15 g/½ oz pink Half and Half into a ball and then into a small sausage shape. Use a little water to attach it to the lungs.

2 Fit a piping bag or baking paper cone with a fine plain piping nozzle and fill with the peach Royal Icing. Pipe branch shapes on the lungs to look like bronchial tubes, and pipe lines on the trachea.

3 For hearts, roll 55 g/2 oz pink Half and Half into a ball. Cut a third off to make the valves. Squeeze the larger amount into a rounded triangle shape for the heart. Roll the smaller amount into a thin sausage and cut into thirds. Use a little water to attach the valves to the top of the heart.

4 Fit 2 piping bags or baking paper cones with fine plain piping nozzles and fill one with the red Royal Icing and the other with the blue Royal Icing. Pipe red and blue branching lines on the heart to appear like veins and arteries.

5 For intestines, roll 25 g/1 oz pink Half and Half into a ball and then into a long, thin sausage. Curve into a squiggly mass, with one end pointing up and one end pointing down, like the beginning and the end of small intestines. Pipe a little red Royal Icing on top and paint with water to thin it. Leave the organs to dry overnight.

6 Preheat the oven to 180°C/160°C fan/ 350°F/Gas Mark 4. Line a 12-hole muffin tin with 12 large paper baking cases. Put the oil, eggs, sugar and vanilla extract in a large bowl and, using an electric whisk, beat together until combined and smooth.

7 Sift in the flour, bicarbonate of soda, spices and salt and then mix together. Stir in the carrots, walnuts and pineapple. Spoon the mixture into the paper cases. Bake for about 25 minutes, turning once halfway through baking, until well risen and firm to the touch. Transfer to a wire rack and leave to cool.

8 To decorate, on a work surface dusted with cornflour, roll out the red, black and purple fondant. Using a 6.5–7.5-cm/ 2½–2⅞-inch round cutter, cut out 4 rounds of each and use to cover the cupcakes. Use a little water to attach the lungs to the red rounds, the hearts to the black rounds and intestines to the purple rounds.

9 Fit a piping bag or baking paper cone with a fine plain piping nozzle and fill with clear piping gel. Pipe the gel all around the edge of each organ to make them appear as if they are oozing.

know your zombie

Seth Grahame-Smith's 2009 book adds zombies to which Jane Austen novel?

1 *Sense and Sensibility*

2 *Mansfield Park*

3 *Pride and Prejudice*

(The answer is on page 80.)

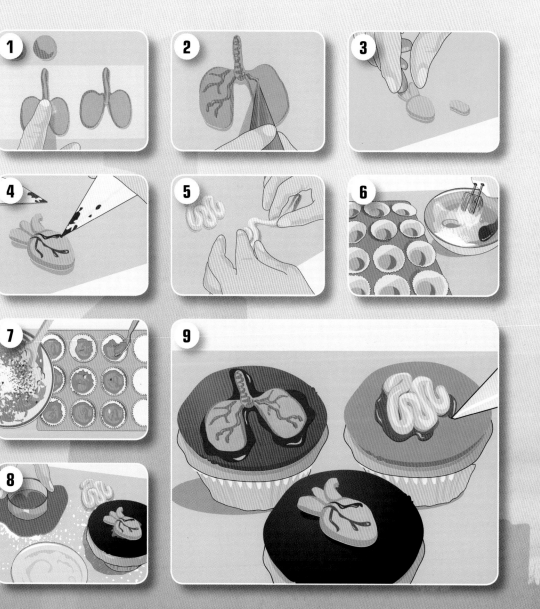

DIFFICULTY RATING

MAKES **12**

Make the decorations the day before baking

bride's
cupcakes

- 1 quantity Vanilla Cupcakes (see Zombie Trick or Treat, page 42)

decorations

- 115 g/4 oz white coverture chocolate
- 24 mini shortbread rounds
- 55 g/2 oz Half and Half, coloured black with 4 drops black paste food colouring (see page 11)
- 50 g/1¾ oz Royal Icing, coloured black with 4 drops black paste food colouring (see page 10)
- 50 g/1¾ oz Royal Icing, coloured yellow with 1 drop yellow paste food colouring
- 48 white sugar pearls or a little white Royal Icing
- 40 g/1½ oz Piping Gel 'Blood' (see page 10)
- 12 marshmallows
- 1.2 kg/2 lb 10 oz plain white Half and Half
- cornflour, for dusting
- 25 g/1 oz plain white Royal Icing
- 12 Knives (see page 15)

bride
&
groom

Even zombies are looking for a match made in Heaven (well, Hell). These two might have found rotting, decrepit love in each other's bloodshot empty eyes, if only the bride could have controlled herself just a little bit longer. Snack on the groom's head before taking a bite out of the scrumptious bride yourself. Retribution is only fair. The bride is made up of an upside-down vanilla cupcake with a marshmallow body and a shortbread head, all secured using a bamboo skewer (remember to let your guests know). Her dress is white Half and Half; don't worry if you tear it – the old superstition about it meaning the marriage will be ended by death doesn't really apply here.

bride & groom

1 Preheat the oven to 180°C/160°C fan/ 350°F/Gas Mark 4. Line a 12-hole muffin tin with 12 large paper baking cases. Make the Vanilla Cupcakes as described in steps 1 and 2 on page 42, but divide all of the mixture between the 12 cupcake cases. Transfer to a wire rack and leave to cool overnight.

2 To make the decorations, melt the chocolate in a microwave oven on Low or in a heatproof bowl set over a saucepan of gently simmering water. Attach a 10-cm/ 4-inch long bamboo skewer to the back of 12 shortbread rounds with a small amount of the melted chocolate. When set, turn the cookies over and spoon the chocolate over the surface to coat evenly. Coat a second set of 12 cookies, without sticks, for the groom. Leave to set. Roll out the Half and Half to make the grooms ties (see page 11) using a strip of acetate 7.5 x 7.5 cm/ 3 x 3 inches. Cut out 2 small triangles to make each tie. Leave to dry on the acetate.

3 Fit piping bags or baking paper cones with fine plain piping nozzles, fill with the black and yellow Royal Icing and use to pipe the faces on the bride and groom. Place a white sugar pearl or a small dot of white Royal Icing in the centre of each black eye to create a pupil. When set, use Piping Gel 'Blood' to pipe around the bride's mouth.

4 To make the bride's body, remove the cupcakes from their cases and level the tops with a serrated knife. Turn the cupcakes upside down and place a marshmallow on top of each. Push a bamboo skewer with a cookie attached through the marshmallow into each cupcake until the cookie rests on the marshmallow.

5 To make the bride's dress, roll 55 g/ 2 oz white Half and Half into a ball. On a work surface dusted with cornflour, roll out the ball into a rectangle with rounded edges, measuring about 9 x 21 cm/ 3½ x 8½ inches. Wrap the rectangle around the bride so that it overlaps at the back and attach with water. Use a craft knife to trim the front so that it tucks under the bride's chin and the base so that it just touches the ground. If wished, make cuts and scrapes in the dress so that it appears tattered.

6 To make the sleeves, roll out 15 g/ 1½ oz of white Half and Half into an oval about 6 x 10 cm/2½ x 4 inches. Cut the oval in half – the straight edges will become the cuffs. Form each half into a cone, leaving a round opening at the wide end. Use water to attach the sides together. Brush water down the seam of each sleeve and attach to the dress. Press the closed end of the sleeve firmly down around the back of the bride.

7 Use white Royal Icing to attach a Knife to one of the sleeves. Pipe Piping Gel 'Blood' on the knife. If wished, use white Royal Icing to pipe details on the dress.

8 To make the veil, roll out 25 g/1 oz white Half and Half very thinly to an oval about 7.5 x 14 cm/3 x 5½ inches. Gather one end together into small pleats and secure the pleats with a little water. Brush water on the back of the pleats, in the centre, and attach the veil to the back of the bride's head so that some of the veil extends above her head. If wished, tatter the veil with a craft knife. Repeat steps 5–8 to make 11 more brides.

9 To assemble, place the bride on the intended display surface. Use white Royal Icing to attach the groom's head to the side of the bride's skirt. Use black Royal Icing to attach the groom's tie to his severed neck. Use Piping Gel 'Blood' to create a pool of blood beneath his tie. Repeat to make the other 11 couples.

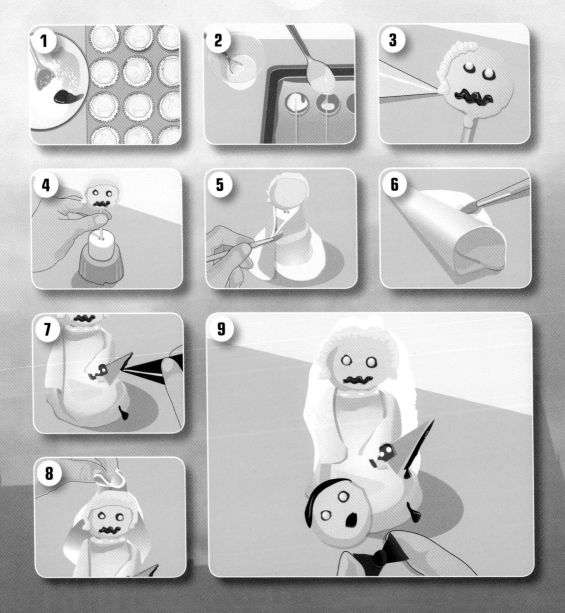

DIFFICULTY RATING

MAKES **12**

Decorations can be made the same day as baking

almond cupcakes

- 2 large eggs
- 125 ml/4 fl oz soured cream
- 1 tsp almond extract
- ¼ tsp pure vanilla extract
- pink paste food colouring
- 250 g/9 oz white plain, cake or pastry flour
- ½ tsp baking powder
- ½ tsp bicarbonate of soda
- ¼ tsp salt
- 25 g/1 oz ground almonds
- 175 g/6 oz granulated sugar
- 175 g/6 oz unsalted butter, softened

In most cases, it is all fun and games until someone loses an eye. This delightfully gory yet delicious almond cupcake is the exception that proves the rule. Be sure to save the eyeball for last to make all your zombie friends jealous as you savour its sweetness. You can replace the blue Half and Half with other colours to vary the colours of the eyes.

decorations

- cornflour, for dusting
- 350 g/12 oz shop-bought fondant, coloured flesh-colour with 2–3 drops peach paste food colouring (see page 11)
- 175 g/6 oz plain white Half and Half (see page 11)
- 175 g/6 oz Half and Half, coloured brown with 10 drops brown and 1 drop black paste food colouring

- 15 g/½ oz Half and Half, coloured blue with 1 drop sky blue paste food colouring
- 10 g/¼ oz Half and Half, coloured black with 1 drop black paste food colouring
- red edible marker pen
- 85 g/3 oz Piping Gel 'Blood' (see page 10)

eye popper

1 Preheat the oven to 180°C/160°C fan/ 350°F/Gas Mark 4. Line a 12-hole muffin tin with 12 large paper baking cases. Put the eggs, 3 tablespoons of the soured cream and the almond and vanilla extracts in a bowl and mix together. Add the pink food colouring in drops or on the end of a cocktail stick and mix well together until evenly coloured deep pink.

2 Sift the flour, baking powder, bicarbonate of soda and salt into a large bowl. Stir in the almonds and sugar. Add the butter and remaining soured cream and, using an electric whisk, beat together until combined. Gradually beat in the egg mixture until combined. Spoon the mixture into the paper cases. Bake for about 20 minutes, turning once halfway through baking, until well risen and firm to the touch. Transfer to a wire rack and leave to cool.

3 When the cupcakes are cold, use your thumb to press an eye socket shape into the top of each.

4 Dust the work surface with cornflour and roll out the fondant to a thickness of 3 mm/⅛ inch. Using a 6.5–7.5-cm/ 2½–2⅞-inch round cutter, cut out 12 rounds that will cover the cupcakes. Press one onto the top of each cupcake.

5 To make the eyeballs, squeeze an eyeball-sized amount from one end of the white Half and Half, then roll it in your fingers to narrow the base. Pull it away from the rest of the Half and Half, and cut with a craft knife so that the eyeball 'stem' is about 2.5 cm/1 inch long. Repeat to make another 11 eyeballs.

6 Divide the brown Half and Half into 12 equal-sized pieces, and roll each piece into a ball. Roll each ball into a sausage shape, flatten and then cut at an angle at one end to create an eyebrow shape. Attach to the cupcake above the eye socket with water.

7 To make the irises for the eyeballs, roll the blue Half and Half out very thinly on a work surface dusted with cornflour. Use the large end of a small plain piping nozzle to cut out 12 x 1-cm/½-inch rounds. Use water to attach one iris to each eyeball. Roll the black Half and Half out very thinly. Use the small end of the nozzle to cut out 12 pupils. Attach a pupil to the centre of each iris with water.

8 Create the appearance of arteries on the eyeballs by drawing on branching lines with the red edible marker pen.

9 Fill the eye sockets with Piping Gel 'Blood'. Sink the 'stem' of an eyeball into the gel in each cupcake and then use water to attach the eyeball to the edge of the cupcake, as if the eyeball has popped out of its socket.

know your
zombie

In the Wolfenstein video games, what is the name of the player's character?

1 Edward Carnby

2 William 'B.J.' Blazkowicz

3 Chris Redfield

(The answer is on page 80.)

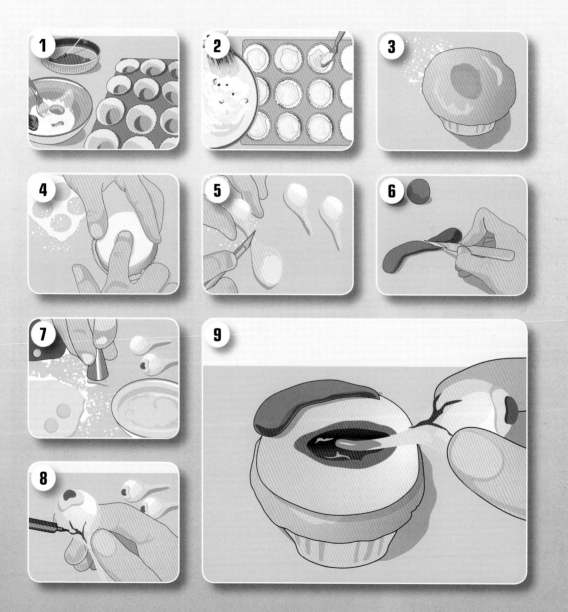

DIFFICULTY RATING

MAKES **12**

Decorations can be made the same day as baking

brain food

honey cupcakes

- 100 g/3½ oz clear honey
- 115 g/4 oz unsalted butter
- 100 g/3½ oz granulated sugar
- 225 g/8 oz white plain, cake or pastry flour
- 1½ tsp baking powder
- ½ tsp ground cinnamon
- ¼ tsp grated nutmeg
- 3 large eggs
- 75 ml/2½ fl oz milk

Brains are a delicacy in the cuisine of many cultures, and zombies are no exception. These sweet honey cupcakes with a delicious buttercream filling are the quintessential end to a big zombie meal. A useful survival tip you should know is that destroying a zombie's brain is a sure-fire way to kill it.

decorations

- 425 g/15 oz Half and Half, coloured pink with 1–2 drops soft pink paste food colouring (see page 11)
- 100 g/3½ oz Royal Icing, coloured peach with 2 drops peach paste food colouring (see page 10)
- ½ quantity Italian Meringue Buttercream (see page 8)
- cornflour, for dusting
- 350 g/12 oz shop-bought fondant, coloured green with 1 drop green and a dab of red paste food colouring (see page 11)
- 115 g/4 oz clear piping gel

brain food

know your zombie

What was the budget for the video of Michael Jackson's 1983 song '*Thriller*'?

1 $100,000

2 $250,000

3 $500,000

(The answer is on page 80.)

1 Preheat the oven to 180°C/160°C fan/ 350°F/Gas Mark 4. Line a 12-hole muffin tin with 12 large paper baking cases. Put the honey, butter and sugar in a large saucepan and heat gently, stirring constantly, until melted and combined. Pour the mixture into a large bowl and leave to cool.

2 Sift the flour, baking powder, salt and spices into the honey mixture and stir together. Using an electric whisk, gradually beat in the eggs and then stir in the milk until smooth. Spoon the mixture into the paper cases. Bake for about 25 minutes, turning once halfway through baking, until well risen and firm to the touch. Transfer to a wire rack and leave to cool.

3 To make the brains, divide the pink Half and Half into 12 equal-sized pieces. Roll one piece into a ball and squeeze it gently from both sides to form an oval. Use the side of the end of a cocktail stick to score a groove down the centre of the oval, creating the 2 hemispheres of the brain. Make sure that the groove curves all the way under the brain. Repeat to make another 11 brains.

4 Fit a piping bag or baking paper cone with a fine plain piping nozzle and fill with the peach Royal Icing. Put each brain on a square of acetate to hold it in place while you are piping, and pipe squiggles and curves all around one side of the brain. Repeat on the other side.

5 To fill the cupcakes, make a large hole in the centre of each cupcake with the handle of a wooden spoon.

6 Fill a piping bag with the Italian Meringue Buttercream and squeeze gently until the hole is filled and a small amount of buttercream comes out of the top.

7 Dust the work surface with cornflour and roll out the green fondant to a thickness of 3 mm/⅛ inch. Using a 6.5–7.5-cm/2½–2⅞-inch round cutter, cut out 12 rounds that will cover the cupcakes. Place a fondant round on the top of each buttercream centre.

8 Use a small amount of water to attach a brain to the centre of each fondant round. Fill a piping bag or baking paper cone fitted with a fine plain piping nozzle with the clear piping gel. Pipe the gel all around the base of each brain to make them look gooey.

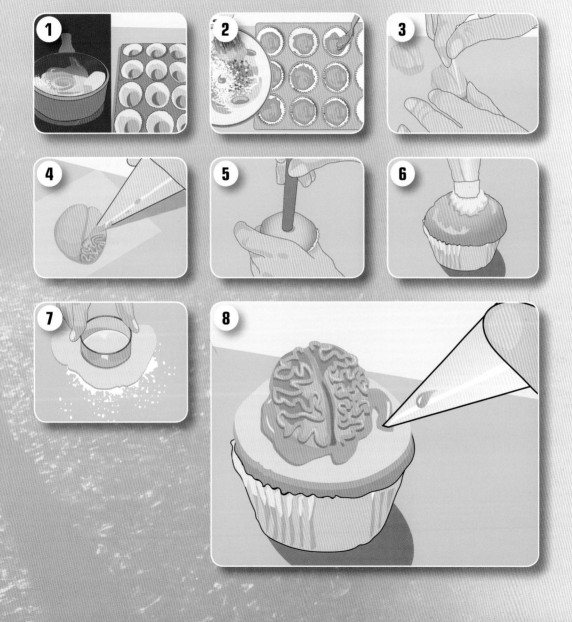

decapitated zombie

DIFFICULTY RATING

MAKES **12**

Decorations can be made the same day as baking

gingerbread cupcakes

- 90 ml/3 fl oz milk
- ¾ tsp bicarbonate of soda
- 125 g/4½ oz unsalted butter, softened
- 100 g/3½ oz soft dark brown sugar
- 90 g/3 oz black treacle or dark molasses
- 3 large eggs, beaten
- 170 g/5¾ oz white plain, cake or pastry flour
- 3 tsp ground ginger
- ¾ tsp ground cinnamon

decorations

- 12 marshmallows
- 225 g/8 oz white couverture or cooking chocolate
- 36 white hard mint sweets
- 175 g/6 oz Piping Gel 'Blood' (see page 10)
- 225 g/8 oz Royal Icing, coloured black with 18 drops black paste food colouring; or brown with 36 drops brown paste colouring; or yellow with 4 drops yellow paste food colouring (see page 10)
- 12 Knives (see page 15; optional)

Imagine you are cornered by a zombie in your kitchen. If you have any hopes of surviving, your best bet is to grab the nearest butcher's knife and take a good swing. This heavenly gingerbread cupcake illustrates what a proud survivor might do after they've fought off the zombie's attack: display the severed head and brag. The head is made from a marshmallow dipped in melted white couverture – good quality coating chocolate with a high percentage of cocoa butter.

pitated

know your zombie

In Night of the Living Dead (1968), the hero Tom hacks up a zombie hand with a kitchen knife. What was this prop made from?

1 Clay filled with chocolate syrup

2 A rubber glove filled with tomato sauce

3 A medical prosthetic filled with real blood

(The answer is on page 80.)

1 Preheat the oven to 160°C/150°C fan/ 325°F/Gas Mark 3. Line a 12-hole muffin tin with 12 large paper baking cases. Put the milk in a bowl and stir in the bicarbonate of soda until dissolved.

2 Put the butter and sugar in a large bowl and, using an electric whisk, beat together until pale and fluffy. Beat in the treacle or molasses and then gradually beat in the eggs. Sift the flour and spices into the mixture and beat together, then gradually beat in the milk mixture. Spoon the mixture into the paper cases. Bake for about 25 minutes, turning once halfway through baking, until firm to the touch. Transfer to a wire rack and leave to cool.

3 For the heads, snip the corners off the top edge of each marshmallow using scissors and then cut into a domed shape. Insert a cocktail stick into the bottom of each marshmallow.

4 Melt the chocolate, stirring every 15 seconds, in a microwave oven on Low or in a heatproof bowl set over a saucepan of gently simmering water. Dip the marshmallows into the melted chocolate up to the flat edge, allowing any extra chocolate to drip back into the bowl.

5 Stick a head-topped cocktail stick into each cooled cupcake so that it stands upright and leave to set. Meanwhile, put a small amount of chocolate on a mint sweet and attach it to one head, just above the bottom edge, for a nose. Repeat for the other heads.

6 Use the tip of a craft knife to drill 2 eye sockets through the chocolate coating just above and on either side of the nose, making the holes slightly larger than the diameter of a mint sweet. Press a mint sweet into each eye socket. When set, remove the head-topped cocktails sticks from the cupcakes. Re-melt the leftover chocolate, dip the top of each cupcake into the chocolate and leave to set.

7 When set, fill a piping bag or baking paper cone fitted with a fine plain piping nozzle with Piping Gel 'Blood' and pipe a pool of dripping blood on each cupcake, for the severed head to sit on. Remove the cocktail sticks from the heads and then place in the blood.

8 Use black, brown or yellow Royal Icing and the fine nozzle to pipe eyebrows and hair on the decapitated head. If wished, smear a Knife with Piping Gel 'Blood' and attach to each cupcake in front of the severed head.

skeletal zombies

DIFFICULTY RATING

MAKES **12**

Make the decorations the day before baking

chocolate mint cupcakes

- 115 g/4 oz unsalted butter, softened
- 200 g/7 oz granulated sugar
- 3 large eggs, beaten
- 150 ml/5 fl oz milk
- 1 tsp mint extract
- 200 g/7 oz white plain, cake or pastry flour
- 20 g/¾ oz cocoa powder
- 1½ tsp baking powder
- ¼ tsp salt
- 100 g/3½ oz mini plain chocolate chips

decorations

- 175 g/6 oz plain white Half and Half (see page 11)
- white vegetable fat, for greasing
- about 120 white hard mint sweets
- 1 quantity Dark Chocolate Ganache (see page 9)
- edible black marker pen (optional)
- 12 Knives (see page 15)
- 20 g/¾ oz Piping Gel 'Blood' (see page 10)

Since zombies are already undead, killing them again isn't easy. One of the less well-known techniques for surviving a zombie attack is to sever your zombie assailant's spinal cord. This minty, chocolatey delight gives you pointers on where exactly to insert the knife. Each cupcake is topped by a generous swirl of chocolate ganache. The head is attached to the cupcake with a cocktail stick, so be sure to warn your guests to remove the cocktail stick before they take a bite.

skeletal zombies

1 The day before, make the decorations. Using 85 g/3 oz Half and Half, roll 2 x 5-mm/¼-inch balls and 2 x 1-cm/½-inch balls for each cupcake, to create the pelvis (you will have some Half and Half left over for the skulls). Roll out the larger balls into ovals and press them flat on to two strips of acetate, each 10 x 27.5 cm/4 x 11 inches (see page 11). Using a paintbrush, paint the facing edges of the 2 flat ovals with water and press together so that they are attached and the ovals narrow at the bottom.

2 Paint the bottoms of the ovals with water. Press the 2 small balls flat below the joined ovals to form the bottom of the pelvic bone. The icing shape should resemble a butterfly at this stage.

3 Paint water in the centre of the pelvic bone, and press on 2–3 mint sweets, side by side, to create the base of the spinal column. Using the small end of a medium plain piping nozzle, cut 4 holes from the pelvic bone. Repeat to make another 11 pelvic bones.

4 To make the skulls, roll 12 ovals from the remaining Half and Half. Use a craft knife to cut part-way into each oval, about a third of the way up, to create the mouth. Use the piping nozzle again to indent circles for eyes. With the blunt end of a cocktail stick, make an indentation below the eyes to create the nose. If wished, use the black edible marker pen to paint in the eyes. Gently push a cocktail stick into the base of each skull and leave the decorations to dry overnight.

5 Preheat the oven to 180°C/160°C fan/ 350°F/Gas Mark 4. Line a 12-hole muffin tin with 12 large paper baking cases. Put the butter and sugar in a large bowl and, using an electric whisk, beat together until pale and fluffy. Gradually beat in the eggs and then stir in the milk and mint extract.

6 Sift the flour, cocoa powder, baking powder and salt into the mixture and then fold in using a large wooden spoon. Spoon the mixture into the paper cases. Sprinkle the chocolate chips over the tops of the cupcakes. Bake for about 25 minutes, turning once halfway through baking, until well risen and firm to the touch. Transfer to a wire rack and leave to cool.

7 When the cupcakes are cold, pipe a round swirl of Dark Chocolate Ganache on the top of each. Press the pelvis on one side of the cupcake, and use 6–7 mint sweets, placed side by side, to create a spinal cord.

8 Place the tip of a knife into the ganache at the place where the mint sweets end on each cupcake. Use Piping Gel 'Blood' in a piping bag or baking paper cone fitted with a fine plain piping nozzle to add some gore.

9 Use a cocktail stick to hold the severed skull to the side of each cupcake about 1 cm/½ inch away from the spinal cord, to make it look as if it has dropped off.

know your zombie

Whose mansion does the group take refuge in the film *Zombieland* (2009)?

1 Bill Murray's

2 Dan Aykroyd's

3 Harold Ramis's

(The answer is on page 80.)

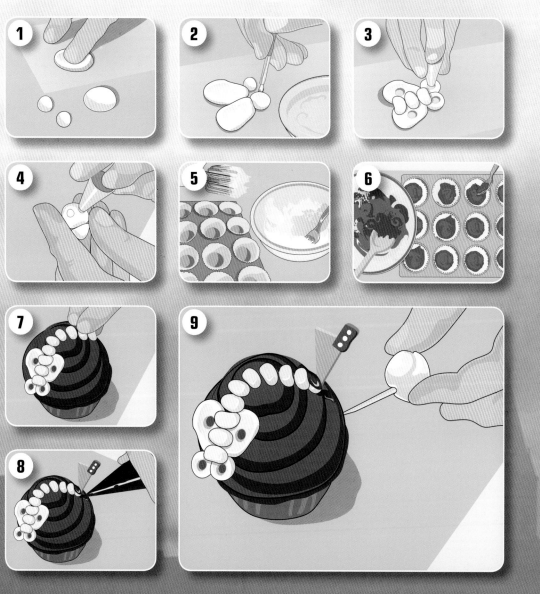

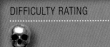

DIFFICULTY RATING

MAKES **12**

Make the decorations the day
before baking

pumpkin cupcakes

- 150 ml/5 fl oz vegetable oil
- 4 large eggs
- 175 g/6 oz granulated sugar
- 200 g/7 oz canned pumpkin
- 225 g/8 oz white plain, cake or pastry flour
- ½ tsp baking powder
- ¼ tsp bicarbonate of soda
- ¼ tsp ground cloves
- ¼ tsp grated nutmeg
- ¾ tsp ground cinnamon
- ¼ tsp salt

bludgeon to survive

In many zombie movies, the heroes have to survive using
whatever improvised instrument they can lay their hands on.
These cupcakes are a little battered from the crowbar, shovel
and baseball bat decorations but, just like you after you've
tasted them, they just keep on coming back for more.

decorations

- 4 Baseball Bats (see page 15)
- 4 Shovels (see page 15)
- 4 Crowbars (see page 15)
- cornflour, for dusting
- 20 g/¾ oz Half and Half, coloured black
  with 2 drops black paste food colouring
  (see page 11)
- 20 g/¾ oz plain white Half and Half
- red edible marker pen
- 50 g/1¾ oz Royal Icing, coloured black
  with 4 drops black paste food colouring
  (see page 10)
- 50 g/1¾ oz plain white Royal Icing

vanilla cream glaze

- 200 g/7 oz icing sugar
- 50 ml/2 fl oz double cream
- 2 tsp pure vanilla extract
- ¼ tsp salt
- 2 drops green paste food colouring
- 1 drop yellow paste food colouring
- 3 drops purple paste food colouring

bludgeon to survive

know your zombie

In the video game *Left 4 Dead 2* (2009), which of these items cannot be used by the players to bludgeon the zombies?

1 Baseball bat

2 Crowbar

3 Shovel

(The answer is on page 80.)

1 The day before, make your weapons – Baseball Bats, Shovels and Crowbars – and leave to dry overnight (see page 15). The following day, make the cupcakes. Preheat the oven to 160°C/150°C fan/325°F/Gas Mark 3. Line a 12-hole muffin tin with 12 large paper baking cases. Put the oil, eggs, sugar and pumpkin in a large bowl and, using an electric whisk, beat together until combined and smooth.

2 Sift in the flour, baking powder, bicarbonate of soda, spices and salt and mix together. Spoon the mixture into the paper cases. Bake for about 25 minutes, turning once halfway through baking, until well risen and firm to the touch. Transfer to a wire rack and leave to cool.

3 When the cupcakes are cold, make the Vanilla Cream Glaze. Put the icing sugar, double cream, vanilla extract and salt in a medium bowl and mix together with a wooden spoon until smooth. Transfer half the mixture to another bowl. Add the green and yellow food colourings to one bowl to colour bright green, and purple food colouring to the other bowl to colour bright purple. Dip 6 cupcakes into the green glaze and the remaining cupcakes into the purple glaze.

4 Press the small end of a medium plain piping nozzle into the glaze repeatedly in a curved shape to make the appearance of a bite mark. Leave the glaze to set for 20 minutes.

5 Dust the work surface with cornflour. Roll the black Half and Half into a ball and then roll out the ball very thinly. Use a craft knife to cut out 12 mouth shapes.

6 Roll the white Half and Half into a ball and roll out very thinly. Use the piping nozzle again to cut out 24 small rounds for eyes.

7 Use the red edible marker pen to add veins to the eyes. Fill a piping bag or baking paper cone fitted with a fine plain piping nozzle with the black Royal Icing and pipe an eyeball in the centre of each eye.

8 Use a small amount of white Royal Icing to attach 2 eyes and a mouth to each cupcake. Use the black Royal Icing to pipe suture lines on one side of the face and to give the zombies mean eyebrows.

9 Fill a piping bag or baking paper cone fitted with a fine plain piping nozzle with the white Royal Icing and use to pipe teeth in the mouth and crossbones on the cupcake cases.

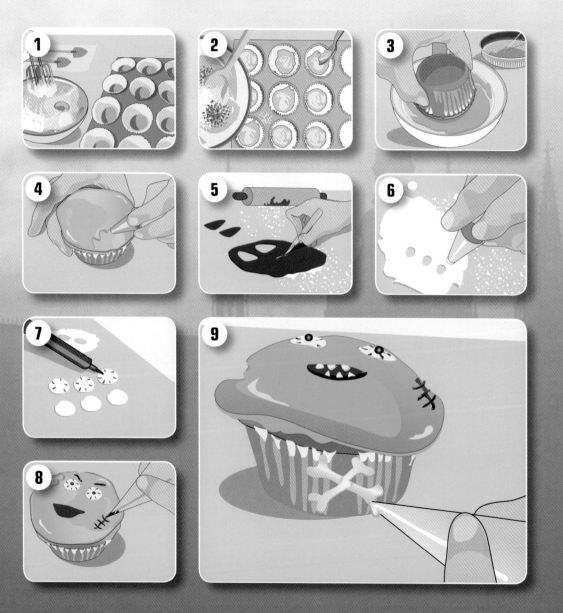

fudge brownie
cupcakes

- 225 g/8 oz plain chocolate
- 85 g/3 oz unsalted butter
- 200 g/7 oz granulated sugar
- 3 large eggs
- 115 g/4 oz white plain, cake or pastry flour
- 20 g/¾ oz cocoa powder
- pinch of bicarbonate of soda
- ¼ tsp salt
- 100 g/3½ oz chopped walnuts

decorations

- 4 Tombstones (see page 13)
- 1 Cross (see page 13)
- 85 g/3 oz Half and Half, coloured black with 5–8 drops black paste food colouring (see page 11)
- ½ quantity Dark Chocolate Ganache (see page 9)
- 2 Rats (see page 14)
- 90 g/3¼ oz chocolate cookie crumbs
- 1 Shovel (see page 15; optional)

graveyard

Beady-eyed rats, fallen crosses and broken tombstones adorn any respectable graveyard. Those who are familiar with zombies know that just because they are buried doesn't mean they will stay buried. These amazing brownie cupcakes create an entire graveyard when arranged together. Add a Shovel (see page 15) filled with cookie crumb earth to make it look like you are still digging a grave.

graveyard

graveyard

know your zombie

Whose grave were the bickering siblings Barbra and Johnny going to visit in the beginning of *Night of the Living Dead* (1968)?

1 Their father's

2 Their mother's

3 Their dog's

(The answer is on page 80.)

1 The day before, make the Tombstones and Cross decorations (see page 13). Also make the fences the day before so that they can dry. Roll out the Half and Half to make the Cupcake Toppers using a strip of acetate 7.5 x 25 cm/3 x 10 inches (see page 11).

2 Using a craft knife, cut the Half and Half into a strip measuring 4.5 x 20 cm/ 1¾ x 8 inches. Make vertical cuts at 8-mm/⅜-inch intervals along the entire length. You will need 16 strips in total.

3 To create a fence section, place 3 black strips, 5 mm/¼ inch apart, on a clean piece of acetate. Cut off the top 2 corners of each strip to create a point.

4 Use a small amount of water to attach a fourth strip at an angle across the 3 pointed fence posts. Repeat with the remaining strips to make 4 fence sections. Leave to dry overnight.

5 Preheat the oven to 180°C/160°C fan/ 350°F/Gas Mark 4. Line a 12-hole muffin tin with 12 large paper baking cases. Break the chocolate into a heatproof bowl set over a saucepan of gently simmering water. Add the butter and heat gently, stirring constantly, until melted and combined. Remove from the heat and leave to cool.

6 Put the sugar and eggs in a large bowl and, using an electric whisk, beat together. Sift in the flour, cocoa powder, bicarbonate of soda and salt and mix together. Add the chocolate mixture and walnuts and stir together. Spoon the mixture into the paper cases. Bake for about 30 minutes, turning once halfway through baking, until the tops are set but the centres still slightly moist. Transfer to a wire rack and leave to cool.

7 To assemble the graveyard, pipe a swirl of Dark Chocolate Ganache onto each cupcake, leaving some of the cupcake showing. Arrange the cupcake in 3 rows of 4. Place a section of fence on each of the cupcakes in the front row.

8 Prop the tombstones on random cupcakes in the back and middle rows at angles; you can break a tombstone cookie and prop it in pieces so that it appears even more decrepit. Place the rats so that they appear to scurry around the gravestones and fence. Cut a slit in one of the cupcakes on the back row and carefully push the cross into it, leaning it at a slight angle.

9 To complete the scene, sprinkle chocolate cookie crumbs around the graveyard to resemble earth. A Shovel also looks great stuck in a cupcake, with extra cookie crumbs, as if it's digging a fresh grave.

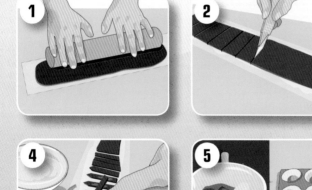

index

trivia answers

p18: 2 Infected lab chimpanzees
p22: 3 The Hive
p26: 1 Wade Davis
p30: 1 The zombies start to die
        of starvation
p34: 1 *Jane Eyre*
p38: 2 Zack Snyder
p42: 2 The Winchester
p46: 1 'I kick ass for the Lord!'

p50: 3 *Pride and Prejudice*
p58: 2 William 'B.J.' Blazkowicz
p62: 3 $500,000
p66: 1 Clay filled with
        chocolate syrup
p70: 1 Bill Murray's
p74: 3 Shovel
p78: 1 Their father's

Acknowledgements

Kitchen equipment supplied by
Premier Gourmet
3465 Delaware Ave
Buffalo, NY 14217
www.premiergourmet.com

*Gourmet facilities for the photoshoot
were provided by*
Artisan Kitchens and Baths
200 Amherst Street
Buffalo, NY 14207
www.artisankitchensandbaths.com